An Appealing Plan

A Year of Everyday Celebrations

Kristina ✓

Celebrate Everyday!

Namarté

Krissy

First Edition Published in the United States of America 2014

www.YellowWelliesMedia.com | www.KraylFunch.com

Library of Congress Cataloging-in-Publication Data available upon request.

ISBN 978-0-9906430-5-0
eISBN 978-0-9906430-0-5

Yellow Wellies Media books may be purchased for educational, business, or promotional use. For information on bulk purchases, please contact the sales department at sales@yellowwelliesmedia.com.

The information in this book is for educational purposes only. Some of the recipes and photographs have appeared in print or digital form.

All photography by Heather Anne Stalker
except where noted in photo credits on page 171

Book design by Crave Creative Group

Editing by Nicole Wayland of Ford Editing

First Edition: October 2014

10 9 8 7 6 5 4 3 2 1

To my mother, Patricia,
for showing me the value of living well and opening your home to others

&

To my husband, Pete,
for teaching me what true love is

Contents

5

Introduction

An Appealing Plan is about celebrating everyday moments, about recognizing the importance of the connection between our surroundings, ourselves, and those around us, about allowing us to feel more in touch with ourselves, our families, and our friends. It's about feeling so inspired by the beauty of the season that we are compelled to redesign our entranceways with containers overflowing with greens or other elements of the season, or to rush home from the market to create a meal using fresh herbs and set a beautiful table with the season's most bountiful flowers whether it's for ourselves or twelve of our closest friends.

It's cliché but true—we spend too much time living virtually and moving so fast that we are rushing past what makes life worth living, like having friends over to share a quick bite or a garden-inspired drink, or creating a multicourse affair designed to allow the conversation of loved ones to marinade and simmer around the table long into the night.

For as long as I can remember, I have dreamed of writing a book to inspire others, to remind them that each and every day can be a celebration of the season, of life, and that it doesn't need to be stressful or complicated to be perfect. Many people I speak with are afraid to entertain. They are intimidated by the images they see in magazines or concerned they might do something wrong, that the entire night will end in a disaster.

In each year, there are 365 days on which to celebrate, and most of us choose the top five or six holidays and leave the rest of the year for the daily routine. But consider what could happen if you chose to celebrate everyday. To find something in each and every day that was special, something in each and every season that inspired you to embrace your home, your surroundings, your friends and family. I'm not suggesting a stress-filled, perfect, June Cleaver kind of celebration or even a Pinterest-perfect party but an everyday table set with care and a menu filled with simply prepared recipes that evoke favorite memories.

I am a gardener at heart, and therefore most of my world is inspired by nature. As you will see throughout the pages of this book, the seasons play an enormous role in my life both inside and outside my home; I'm constantly transitioning what's growing in my garden containers, my recipe selection, and even the pillows on my couch. Plain and simple—I am passionate about beautiful things. I believe that our surroundings affect us immensely, and when we are truly connected to them we are the most content and are able to spread this joy on to others.

Call it a trend or a return to the past, but I believe we are bringing back entertaining at home, lingering over a table after a lovingly prepared meal with friends. It has been a way of life and passion of mine my entire adult life, and I am thrilled to be able to invite you on this journey with me through a year of celebrating every day, taking the time to slow down and honor our relationships, the seasons, and ourselves.

I hope this book will inspire you to see that the world can be a beautiful celebration everyday. Beginning with spring, each section represents a season, offering seasonal decorating ideas followed by menus for gatherings influenced by my childhood, travels, and the season itself.

I encourage you to visit the website {www.AnAppealingPlan.com}, so we can share updates, discussions, recipes, new trends, and, best of all, I have created a shopping list for each gathering in this book, all ready for you to print out and use. Now let's get started—welcome to the celebration called life.

—*Krayl Funch*

Spring

In Bloom

In spring, also known as the awakening, the world finally sheds its winter coat and comes out of hibernation. We throw open the windows to allow the fresh breeze into our homes, and we pull off the heavy bedding and replace it with a lighter summer quilt. The mood changes, and we find ourselves waving to neighbors we haven't seen in months.

In the garden, the ground begins to shift, making room for tiny shoots finally ready to peek through after a long winter underground. We check daily for signs of life, to catch a glimpse of the tips of bulbs planted in the fall or to see if a Peony that struggled last season will return to flower another year. We know that the warmer days and bright sunshine will wake them from the soil, and they will amaze us once again by bringing beauty to our courtyards and walkways.

Early spring branches come alive with tiny blooms, and although we leave some to flower naturally, we can't resist cutting just a few to bring inside before a late cold snap comes to stifle their announcement that spring has arrived.

We celebrate renewal, rebirth, mothers of all sorts, and, of course, good friends. The colors of the world and our surroundings transform from grays and deep browns to pinks and those bright greens we just can't get enough of—this is certainly the preppiest season of them all.

Welcome the beauty of spring into your home by adding natural touches, such as forced hyacinth, paperwhite narcissus, and orange tulip bulbs, to decorate a coffee table. Seemingly small changes to your existing decor that embrace the season connect you to the changes happening outside your windows.

Ahhh, Spring

Even the meals on our tables change from warm and hearty to fresh and crisp—a rainbow of early spring peas, nasturtiums, and baby lettuce is a much-needed and welcome change. Invite friends over for an early dinner to rejoice in the first offerings of the spring season.

Draw back the curtains, open the windows, and let natural light flood the space and brighten the table in a way only spring sunshine can. Your guests' laughter will fill the room and plans for the warmer days will be made to fill your calendar.

Set the table with accent plates of deep robin's egg blue on top of stoneware dinner plates. Grass green water goblets also add a nice touch. Use pottery pitchers to hold tall, puffy clouds of white hydrangeas and an assortment of smaller glass bud vases to hold clippings that will bring life to the lower level of the table.

On the Menu

Spring Pea & Mint Chilled Soup
Wild-Caught Salmon
Oven-Roasted Asparagus
White Wine

Spring Pea & Mint Chilled Soup

The first time I made this recipe was for a family luncheon, and it was such a big hit that it has since become a must-have for any spring gathering. The flavor of the spring peas is so intense, the lemon juice is so bright, and the mint brings just the right touch of freshness. It also freezes well, so consider making a double batch to enjoy later in the week.

Ingredients

Serves 6 to 8

2 tablespoons **unsalted butter**
3 cups **onion, coarsely chopped {approx. 1 large}**
Salt and freshly ground black pepper
4 cups **vegetable broth**
2 cups **water**
6 cups **fresh peas**
3 cups **packed flat-leaf parsley leaves**
1 cup **packed mint leaves**
2 tablespoons **fresh lemon juice**
1/4 cup **crème fraîche, for garnish**
Pea shoots, for garnish

Method

1. Melt butter in a large pot {uncovered} over medium heat. Add onion and 2 teaspoons salt. Cook, stirring occasionally, until onion is translucent, about 5 minutes.

2. Add broth and water, and bring to a boil over high heat. Stir in peas and return to a boil. Remove from heat and stir in roughly chopped parsley and mint.

3. Puree soup in a blender or by using an immersion blender until very smooth.

4. Transfer to a clean bowl and stir in lemon juice.

5. Season to taste with salt and pepper. Chill soup in refrigerator for 1 to 2 hours or overnight.

6. Serve in soup bowls and garnish with crème fraîche and pea shoots.

Wild-Caught Salmon with Oven-Roasted Asparagus

We all have recipes, flavors, and dishes that we could eat almost every meal—mine is salmon with a vegetable side, both lightly seasoned with herbs and citrus. When your ingredients are in season and fresh, it makes a noticeable difference in the flavor. Ask your local fish monger or farmer's market what they recommend; each will become a valuable resource when planning your menu.

Ingredients

Serves 6 to 8

For the salmon:
2 pounds **fresh salmon**
1/2 cup **dry white wine**
1 teaspoon **thyme, finely chopped**
1/2 teaspoon **salt**
1/2 teaspoon **freshly ground black pepper**
1 **lemon, juiced**
Lemon slices, for garnish

For the asparagus:
1 1/2 pounds **asparagus, thin**
Olive oil
Kosher salt
Freshly ground black pepper

Method

1. **Preheat oven to 400°F.**

2. **For the salmon: Combine white wine, thyme, salt, and pepper in a resealable plastic bag. Add salmon and seal bag. Refrigerate 30 minutes, turning occasionally.**

3. **Place salmon on a parchment paper–lined baking sheet. Sprinkle lemon juice evenly over salmon. Lay lemon slices on salmon. Cook for 20 minutes.**

4. **For the asparagus: Cut off the tough white ends of the asparagus.**

5. **Place the asparagus on a baking sheet, drizzle with olive oil, sprinkle with salt and pepper, and then toss to coat the asparagus completely. Spread the asparagus in a single layer and roast for 25 minutes.**

A Baby Shower

It is always a joy to celebrate the arrival of a new baby {no matter the season}; however, spring does carry an intrinsic feeling of newness that adds to this special occasion. The world is bursting at the seams with newness and is ready to welcome a little bundle of joy.

Occasionally, you may feel that the best venue for a particular celebration is outside of the home—maybe a favorite local spot or location that carries a memory for you or your guests. When this is the case, work with the existing décor and keep the overall feel of the gathering in line with the setting you have selected. If the space is airy with lots of natural light, select flowers and material that add a natural element to the table but don't steal the show from existing décor or, most importantly, the guest of honor: our mom-to-be.

Nantucket Blue hydrangeas with Kermit Button mums atop alternating double- and single-stacked white Birchwood block vases add just the right touch of floral whimsy while still keeping the overall feel slightly rustic and truly little boy.

Offer a celebratory cocktail using fresh ingredients to welcome guests, but remember to have a nonalcoholic version available as well. Provide ribbons or charms to convey the different drinks so there is no confusion.

On the Table

Flowers to Coordinate with the Overall Theme
Dessert Table Including Cupcakes & Macaroons
Fresh Lime Cosmopolitan & Cranberry Spritzer

To set the tone of the event, start with the invitation. Then, follow through with the theme using similar colors or patterns. Blue and white chevron carries the pattern of a bow tie on the invitation to a dessert table filled with cupcakes and macaroons. A blue-and-white clothesline with nautical clothing and an anchor-themed diaper cake complete the décor fit for our little man.

Fresh Lime Cosmopolitan & Cranberry Spritzer

I know, I know. Cosmos are so "Sex in the City" and early 90s—right. But they are so pretty and happy! The trick here is to use fresh lime juice; there is no other way around it. The fresh bite of real lime juice makes all the difference in the world. Offer a Cranberry Spritzer for guests who prefer a nonalcoholic version but still would like to enjoy a celebratory beverage.

Ingredients

For the Cosmopolitan:

Makes One Cocktail

1 1/2 ounces **high-quality vodka**
1/2 ounce **Cointreau**
1/2 ounce **cranberry juice, 100% juice**
3/4 ounce **fresh-squeezed lime juice**
1 slice **lime, thin, for garnish**

For the Cranberry Spritzer:

Makes 4 to 6 servings

2 cups **cranberry juice, 100% juice**
2 tablespoons **fresh-squeezed lime juice**
2 1/2 cups **lemon-lime seltzer, chilled**
Ice, **to chill**
Lime slices and frozen cranberries, for garnish

Method

For the Cosmopolitan:

In a cold cocktail shaker filled with ice, combine vodka, Cointreau, lime juice, and cranberry juice. Shake well for 5 to 10 seconds. Strain liquid into a chilled glass. Garnish with a lime slice.

For the Cranberry Spritzer:

To create a mocktail version of the Cosmo, pour cranberry juice and lime juice into a pitcher and stir well. Add seltzer slowly. Pour over ice and garnish with lime slices and cranberries.

Just Between Friends

Planned celebrations, admittedly, can take hours to organize and execute—which I am always delighted to do—but what happens when out of the blue there is a knock on your door, and there stands a neighbor announcing her engagement or new promotion?

A friend of mine says, "Every time I stop by your house, there is a mimosa ready and a beautifully set table." This is a slight exaggeration, but I love that she feels this way. In reality, all it takes is stocking your fridge with a bottle of bubbly and your favorite cheeses, and having fresh flowers from the garden on the table. Once you get in the habit, it becomes second nature.

I am not suggesting that you need to worry about your home being picture perfect all the time, but with a few details in place, you can quickly make your home not only more pleasant for you to live in, but it will also allow you to feel more at ease when the impromptu celebration does arise.

On the Menu

Baked Brie with Almonds & Rosemary Syrup
Raw Honeycomb & Crusty French Bread
Fresh White Peach Bellini

Baked Brie with Almonds, Rosemary Syrup, & Honeycomb

When you first begin entertaining, you will quickly find a few recipes that you love to make and guests are sure to enjoy. For me—right from the start—it was baked Brie. I have made it many ways; however, the addition of rosemary syrup and toasted almonds offers a new contrast in textures and flavors to this classic appetizer.

Ingredients

Serves 8

1 small **wheel of Brie, about 9 ounces**
3 tablespoons **Rosemary Syrup {see below}**
1/2 cup **slivered almonds, toasted**
1 sprig **rosemary, organic, for garnish**
Fresh, raw honeycomb
Crusty french bread to serve

Rosemary Syrup:
1 cup **local fresh honey**
1/3 cup **water**
2 **rosemary sprigs, organic**

Method

1. **For the Rosemary Syrup: In a small pan, heat honey and water on low heat until it is thin and fully combined. Add rosemary sprig to honey mixture and stir to coat rosemary. Heat on low for an additional 15 minutes. Remove from heat and allow mixture to cool slightly.**

2. **Use immediately or store in an airtight container until you are ready to use.**

3. **For the Brie: Preheat oven to 350°F. Line a baking tray with parchment paper.**

4. **Using a sharp knife, remove the top rind on cheese wheel, being careful not to remove the sides. Place on tray. Bake cheese for 15 to 20 minutes, until softened.**

5. **Remove cheese from oven. Place on serving platter alongside honeycomb and bread. Slowly drizzle warmed Rosemary Syrup onto the top. Top with the toasted almonds and rosemary sprig, and serve immediately.**

Fresh White Peach Bellini & Citrus Mimosa

It has been true love between the Bellini and me since my first sweet sip at the bar at Balthazar in New York City. To me, it is the upscale cousin of the mimosa, slightly less sweet and appealing to those wishing to sip and savor the flavor of the prosecco.

You can purchase peach puree in speciality stores, but try making your own fresh at least once.

Ingredients

Serves 6 to 8

For the Bellini:

4 ripe **white peaches, peeled, seeded, diced**
2 teaspoons **sugar**
1 bottle **chilled prosecco or champagne**

For the Mimosa:

8 to 10 large **in-season oranges, juiced**
1 bottle **champagne or prosecco**

Citrus Suggestions:
  Winter: Navel
  Summer: Valencia

Method

For the White Peach Bellini:

1. **Place the peaches and sugar in the bowl of a food processor and process until smooth. Press the mixture through a sieve and discard the peach solids. Chill until ready to use.**

2. **Place 2 teaspoons of the peach puree into each champagne flute and fill slowly with cold prosecco. Serve immediately.**

For the Citrus Mimosa:

1. **Fill chilled glasses halfway with champagne. Slowly top with fresh juice. Serve cold.**

{Note: The amount of juice from each fruit will vary, so adjust quantity based on results. Select an in-season variety to ensure highest volume of juice.}

Mother's Day Brunch

Mother's Day, or Mothering Sunday, as it is referred to in England, is a relatively young holiday in American history, dating back to the 1870s, which is surprising considering mothers have been loved and celebrated much longer than that!

Of course we should honor and thank our mothers every day of the year; however, on this particular day, they should be treated extra special. Flowers and pretty details abound on this occasion, which also reminds us that it is finally safe to plant again in the garden without the danger of frost damaging those tender leaves.

Re-create the emerging spring energy inside by decorating your table with vibrant floral-patterned dinnerware, cut flower arrangements in glossy, pale blue flowerpots bursting with Mom's favorite flowers, and a menu that embraces the season.

On the Menu

Spinach & Gruyere Quiche
Wild Rice Salad
Mixed Greens with Edible Flowers
Sparkling Cranberry Spritzer {see page 25}

Spinach & Gruyere Quiche

When I was in college, I worked at a café where we baked and sold multiple varieties of quiche, completely selling out of them all each day. I am still friendly with a few girlfriends who worked there, and to this day they tease me about the fact that I "taught" them how to make quiche from a carton. We have all moved on from the café, and I have mended my foolish ways {thanks to the guidance of Julia Child}, but I still love quiche and serve one anytime I am hosting a brunch.

Quiches are great warm or cold, and, contrary to popular belief, even the men will love it! Spinach and cheese is a classic variety, but I prefer Gruyere over the traditional Swiss, as the flavor is much milder.

Ingredients

Makes one 9-inch quiche

1 9-inch **pie crust**
2 tablespoons **butter**
2 tablespoons **minced shallots**
2 cups **blanched spinach, chopped**
1/2 teaspoon **salt**
1 1/2 cups **grated Gruyere cheese**
3 large **eggs**
1 1/2 cups **whipping cream**
1/8 teaspoon **freshly ground black pepper**
Pinch of nutmeg

Method

1. **Preheat oven to 375°F.**

2. **Bake 9-inch pie crust for 10 to 15 minutes, or until it just starts to turn golden brown. Set aside to cool.**

3. **In a medium saucepan, melt butter and cook shallots briefly on medium heat. Add spinach. Stir and cook over medium heat until water has evaporated. Stir in salt. Taste, and adjust seasoning if necessary.**

4. **Sprinkle half of the cheese over the bottom of the pie crust and top with spinach mixture. Sprinkle the remaining cheese over the top.**

5. **Beat eggs, cream, pepper, and nutmeg in mixing bowl.**

6. **Pour the custard mixture into the pie crust, and bake at 375°F for 30 to 40 minutes, or until the edges are set but the quiche still jiggles a little in the center.**

7. **Cool for at least 15 minutes before serving.**

Wild Rice Salad

Wild rice is a much healthier alternative to pasta but still satisfies that carb craving. This recipe produces a visually appealing dish full of textures and flavors. It works well as a side dish with vegetables just as well as with a protein.

Dried cranberries add a tart flavor, but try various dried fruits when the season allows for it.

Ingredients

Serves 8 to 10

1 cup **wild rice**
3/4 cup **chopped walnuts, toasted**
1 cup **celery, finely chopped**
1/2 cup **dried cranberries, chopped**
1 scallion **{white and green parts}, chopped**
1/2 cup **parsley leaves, finely chopped**
5 tablespoons **vegetable or walnut oil**
4 tablespoons **lemon juice**
1/2 teaspoon **salt, plus more**
1/4 teaspoon **freshly ground black pepper, plus more**

Method

1. **Put wild rice, 4 cups of water, and 1 teaspoon of salt in a large pot. Bring to a boil. Reduce heat to maintain a simmer, partially cover, and cook until the wild rice is tender, 45 to 60 minutes. Drain the rice if water remains and set aside to cool slightly.**

2. **In a large bowl, combine wild rice, walnuts, celery, dried cranberries, and scallions.**

3. **In a small bowl, combine parsley, oil, lemon juice, salt and pepper. Pour liquid mixture over ingredients in large bowl and combine. Season, to taste, with salt and pepper.**

4. **Chill overnight and remove 30 minutes prior to serving. Serve at slightly chilled or room temperature.**

{Note: To toast nuts, heat a large, dry {unoiled} pan on the stovetop on medium heat. When the pan is hot, add a single layer of nuts. Stir frequently with a wooden spoon until the nuts turn golden brown and you can smell their aroma. Use immediately.}

Mixed Greens with Edible Flowers

Food and flowers have been natural partners in our gardens and on our tables for ages, but most don't realize that they can be partners on our plates as well. Edible flowers, with their vibrant colors, compelling scents, and lovely shapes, can provide beautiful accents for decorating a plate. When you're choosing an edible flower, consider how to complement the food's appearance as well as the flavors; most flowers work well with salads, but take more care using them in desserts and cocktails.

Organic Edible Flowers

Basil: **Blossoms come in a variety of colors, from white to pink to lavender; flavor is similar to the leaves but milder; combination of peppermint and fresh Italian basil flavor.**

Bachelor's Button: **Spiky-looking but soft; can be blue, purple, pink, rose, or white; flavor is similar to a cucumber, and it has a fun, frilly texture.**

Chive: **Hardy perennial, blooms in the early spring; purple flower heads made up of individual florets that can be used whole or broken off and added to salads; garlicky-onion flavor.**

Dill: **Flowers are white to yellow in small umbels; flavor similar to leaves but stronger.**

Marigold: **Blossoms range in color from orange to golden yellow; alluring fragrance and sweet citrus taste works well with sweet or savory dishes; adds acidity to leafy green salads.**

Mint: **Flowers are white to purple; minty taste with flowery overtones.**

Nasturtium: **The tastiest flower; peppery and mustardy with a touch of honey; ranges from yellow to reddish-orange.**

Sage: **Grayish leaves and blue to purplish flowers; subtle sage flavor.**

Snapdragon: **Wide range of colors: yellow, pink, deep pink, white; bland-to-bitter flavor.**

Pansy: **The largest of the viola-type flowers, all of which are edible {smallest are Johnny-jump-ups}; faint lettuce-like taste; velvety texture.**

Cinco de Mayo

Some holidays are purely about the celebration of good food, great friends, and the season, and Cinco de Mayo is just one of those days. Frequently misunderstood and thought to be a celebration of independence, it has become more of a fun holiday celebrating the Mexican way of life rather than about remembering a battle that happened over 150 years ago in the city of Puebla.

The atmosphere for the day is lighthearted and upbeat; no presents or over-the-top décor are required. To set the mood, simply put on festive music, place banana leaves or palm fronds with brightly colored flowers down the table instead of a table linen, and add a few thoughtfully placed lanterns to light up the path as sunset approaches.

It is a great opportunity to encourage your guests to make and bring their favorite dish to complete the menu. As the host, offer a few key elements, like a refreshing herb-infused cocktail along with an appetizer and main dish option, then make sure there is room for those extra dishes on the table. Entertaining in this style allows you to make items the night before, with little to no prep the day of, so you will be able to relax and enjoy the company.

On the Menu

Grilled Fish Tacos
Homemade Guacamole
Cilantro-Lime Mojito

Grilled Fish Tacos & Homemade Guacamole

Fish tacos came into my life way too late. When I cut back my consumption of red meat, ground beef was the first to go, and therefore tacos as I knew them were off my menu. But then this delicious alternative appeared: blackened fish on soft, flour tortillas, topped with fresh herbs, vegetables, salty cheese, and fresh crème—it is the perfect meal to enjoy on a warm day with a cold beverage and good friends.

Ingredients

Serves 6

1 1/2 pounds **flaky white fish {tilapia, bass, grouper}**
1/4 cup **canola oil**
1 **lime, juiced**
1 tablespoon **ancho chili powder**
1/4 cup **fresh cilantro leaves, chopped**
1/2 teaspoon **salt**
1/4 teaspoon **freshly ground black pepper**
12 **flour tortillas**

Guacamole:
2 large **cloves garlic, chopped**
1/2 teaspoon **kosher salt**
3 tablespoons **freshly squeezed lime juice**
3 **avocados, halved, seeded, and peeled**
1 small **red onion, diced**
2 **Roma tomatoes, seeded and diced**
2 tablespoons **cilantro, chopped**
Freshly ground black pepper, to taste

Toppings:
Red cabbage, 1 medium, shredded
Crème or queso fresco
Red onion, thinly sliced
Green onion, thinly sliced
Cilantro, whole or hand-torn
Lime wedges

Method

1. Preheat grill on medium-high heat.

2. Place fish in a medium-sized dish. In a small bowl, whisk together the oil, lime juice, ancho powder, cilantro, and salt and pepper, and pour over the fish. Set aside to marinate for 15 to 20 minutes.

3. Remove fish from marinade and place onto a hot grill. Grill the fish for 4 minutes on the first side, then, turning once, cook for about 7 to 8 minutes total. The fish should be opaque in the center. Let rest for 5 minutes, then flake the fish with a fork into chunks.

4. Stack and wrap the tortillas in aluminum foil and place on the grill away from the direct heat and grill for 1 to 2 minutes to warm.

5. Divide the fish among the tortillas and garnish with any or all of the garnishes. Serve with lime wedges.

6. For the guacamole: Using a mortar and pestle, grind garlic and salt together to form a paste. Add lime juice and mix. In a large bowl, place the avocado, transfer salt and lime juice, and toss to coat. Fold in the onion, tomatoes, and cilantro. Let sit for 30 minutes and serve.

44

Cilantro-Lime Mojito

I once took an informal survey over the course of a year, asking people for their thoughts on cilantro and ginger in an attempt to determine whether people had a preference. The results were inconclusive, but I have found that when it comes to cilantro, most people either love it or could leave it. Me? I love it. This cocktail is a celebration of herbs and citrus, and the fun you can have when you embrace the bounty of the season. Cheers.

Ingredients

Makes one cocktail

2 tablespoons **fresh cilantro leaves**
2 tablespoons **fresh lime juice {about 1 lime}**
2 tablespoons **Cilantro Simple Syrup {see below}**
2 ounces **white rum**
Club soda
1 **lime wedge, for garnish**

Cilantro Simple Syrup:
2 cups **sugar**
1 cup **water**
20 **cilantro stems, roughly chopped**

Method

1. **First, make the Cilantro Simple Syrup. Combine the sugar with water in a small saucepan and bring to a simmer over medium-high heat. Once simmering, stir until the sugar dissolves, then remove from heat. Add the cilantro muddle to allow flavors to infuse. Cool, at least 15 minutes. Strain out the stems and then store the syrup in the refrigerator in an airtight container.**

2. **Muddle the cilantro with the lime juice and Cilantro Simple Syrup in a cocktail shaker. Add 1 cup ice and top with rum. Cover and shake well. Pour into glass without straining. Top with a splash of club soda, and garnish with a lime wedge on the rim of the glass.**

Summer

Summer Lovin'

You know how a mother is not supposed to let her children know which one is her favorite? Well, that's how I feel about summer. I love all the seasons for what they offer, but when I am being honest about it, summer is my favorite, and I am pretty sure she knows it.

Perhaps it's the seductive combination of the long days and warm nights mixed with fresh-cut herbs and seasonal produce, all brought together with good friends over the course of a three-day weekend—eating outside, lingering around a flickering candle, creating memories that last until the warmth of next year, memories that last a lifetime.

Or maybe it is the weekends spent at my aunt's beach house waking up to the sound of seagull chatter, fresh coffee brewing, and the excitement of getting down to the water to set up the perfect spot on the beach to spend the afternoon reading and listening to the waves crash, then returning home to enjoy a feast at the picnic table, hours of cracking crab and telling stories long into the night.

My connection to nature seems more intense than ever during this time of year. I love to see the entranceways of homes in the neighborhood come alive with garden containers full of the brightest yellows, blues, and greens of the season's flowers combined with fresh herbs seeming to almost wave hello as you walk by. Or heading into the garden to pick ripe tomatoes, eggplants, and peppers, and only then deciding what will be on the menu. Is there anything more fulfilling than creating a meal with produce that you grew from seed, cared for, and checked on daily until that moment when it is ready to be picked?

When arranging flowers, your vessel is just as important as the flowers in determining the shape and feel of the final arrangement. During the summer months, I frequently use lined terra-cotta pots to mimic the feel of the outdoor garden.

Begin by creating a base that will support the height and shape of the selected varieties. Oasis, a floral frog, or even pebbles will do the trick. Placing the fuller flowers in first will fill larger openings and begin to form a natural shape. Finish by adding taller flowers to add height.

Peonies and snapdragons are the perfect combination for a summer arrangement. They remind me of an English garden path, peaking through the fence, with their multiple blooms and naturally curved stems. They both come in a variety of colors, and each is as lovely as the next.

Summer Solstice

It is the longest day of the year and fabled to hold mystical powers of fertility and abundance. Farmers plan their crops around it, and couples schedule taking their vows based on this day. Whether you are a gardener or a soon-to-be newlywed, I advise you to take advantage of the longer daylight to schedule a celebration outside among nature, perhaps even set in the garden. Incorporate the colors of summer into your celebration by using a colorfully patterned tablecloth, and bring out your summer dinnerware and festive glassware. Place an overflowing flower arrangement in the center of the table, and let the flavors of freshly picked herbs fill the menu.

Luckily, there is no official rule stating that every gathering needs to have multiple courses, so a one-dish menu is perfect for lunch or as a first course before moving onto the main course.

A pretty table deserves a cocktail that is equally attractive. Herb-based cocktails bring out and compliment the flavors in your meal. Look toward the garden to create a refreshing beverage that lures you to stay in the garden all night.

On the Menu

Bobo's Mead with Lavender Honey
Orzo Salad

Bobo's Meade with Lavender Honey

Every spring, I watch the lavender plants in my garden grow into dreamy-smelling, blue-gray mounds and wait for their purple flowers to burst out and announce that summer has finally arrived. When they do, I grab a few blooms and whip up a batch of my lavender honey. It is perfect on scones, with cheese, and in cocktails.

Ingredients

Makes one cocktail

3 ounces **high-quality gin**
2 tablespoons **Lavender Honey {see below}**
2 tablespoons **lime juice, freshly squeezed**
Tonic water, chilled
Ice
Lavender flowers, for garnish
Lavender sprig, for garnish

Lavender Honey:
1/4 cup **lavender flowers, organic or culinary**
2 cups **local fresh honey**

Method

1. First, prepare the Lavender Honey. In a small pan, heat honey on low heat until it is thin and slides off a metal spoon easily. Add lavender flowers to honey and stir to combine. Heat on low for an additional 5 minutes, stirring continuously. Do not allow to boil.

2. Remove from heat and allow mixture to cool slightly.

3. Using a fine strainer or cheese cloth, pour the honey into an airtight container to store until you are ready to use.

4. Combine gin, Lavender Honey, and lime juice into a cocktail shaker filled with ice. Shake well to chill.

5. Add ice to a low glass. Strain over ice, add a splash of tonic water, sprinkle with lavender flowers, and garnish with a lavender sprig.

{Note: This recipe is my variation of a cocktail served at one of my favorite restaurants in New York. Quantities and actual ingredients may vary in their version.}

Orzo Salad

Orzo salad is one of my favorite items to make and bring to a gathering. You can make it the day before and add almost anything from your pantry, and it is sure to be a hit! This combination is bright, tangy, and perfect as a vegetarian main dish or as a side dish to any menu.

Ingredients

Serves 6 to 8

Vinaigrette:
1/4 cup **red wine vinegar**
3 tablespoons **fresh lemon juice**
1 teaspoon **honey**
1/3 cup **olive oil**
1 tablespoon **lemon zest**
Salt and freshly ground black pepper

Salad:
12 ounces **orzo pasta**
6 cups **broth {chicken or vegetable}**
2 cups **grape or cherry tomatoes, halved**
1/2 cup **red onion, diced**
3 tablespoons **fresh flat-leaf parsley, chopped**
1 cup **feta cheese, crumbled**
1/2 cup **pine nuts, toasted**
Salt and freshly ground black pepper

Method

1. **For the vinaigrette: Whisk together the vinegar, lemon juice, honey, and oil. Season to taste with a bit of salt and pepper. Set aside.**

2. **For the salad: Cook the orzo in the chicken broth until tender, according to package directions. Drain well. Add 1 to 2 tablespoons of dressing to pasta to avoid sticking. Set aside until pasta cools to room temperature.**

3. **Toss the cooled pasta with the tomatoes, onions, and parsley.**

4. **Pour the vinaigrette over the salad and stir to coat with the dressing. Season with salt and pepper, to taste. Add feta and pine nuts over the top and toss lightly. Serve at room temperature.**

{Note: If making this salad the day before, reserve 1/3 of the dressing and pine nuts to add right before serving.}

Brunch for Two

Never dismiss the value of a quiet meal between two people. Before I was married, I would watch couples who could sit through the majority of a meal without talking to each other, reading the paper or writing some list. I thought, "I never want to be that kind of couple; they must be so bored." Turns out, I now actually look forward to sitting with my husband reading the paper, sharing or commenting, then returning to quietly reading my paper.

A quiet brunch allows you to enjoy the remainder of the weekend, connect through conversation, and relax before the rush of the week sets in again. The best part of brunch is that there is no rush; the day lies ahead, and the meal is meant to be savored. Put on serene background music to encourage lingering and light conversation.

Keep the table open for papers, magazines, and extra cups of coffee. A small bud vase filled with clippings from the garden like dusty miller, green trick, and a lavender sprig add a touch of nature and a variety of textures.

On the Menu

Savory Herb Waffles with Smoked Salmon
Perfectly Poached Eggs
Fresh-Squeezed Citrus Mimosa {see page 32}

Savory Herb Waffles, Smoked Salmon, & Poached Egg

Perhaps it is my time spent in the South that inspired my first batch of savory waffles, or maybe it was that extra bunch of herbs staring at me from the counter, just asking to be used up. Either way, I am glad I did it, as they are now a permanent fixture in my recipe collection. Feel free to mix and match herbs to your taste and seasonal availability.

Ingredients

Serves 8

2 cups **unbleached all-purpose flour**
2 teaspoons **baking powder**
1 1/2 teaspoons **kosher salt**
2 large **eggs**
2 cups **whole milk**
4 tablespoons **melted, unsalted butter, as needed**
1 tablespoon **fresh thyme, finely chopped**
1 tablespoon **fresh tarragon, finely chopped**
8 ounces **smoked salmon, very thinly sliced**
Poached eggs
Salt and freshly ground black pepper

Method

1. **While your waffle iron preheats, mix the dry ingredients in a large bowl, then blend with a whisk to break up lumps.**

2. **In a separate bowl, whisk together eggs, milk, and melted butter. Stir in thyme. Stir wet ingredients into dry ingredients and mix until thoroughly combined.**

3. **Let batter rest for at least 5 minutes before cooking according to waffle iron instructions. Keep waffles warm in a preheated oven on a cookie sheet, one layer deep.**

4. **For poached eggs: Gently simmer 2 to 3 inches of water in a saucepan. Add one tablespoon of vinegar per quart of water. Break a fresh egg and, holding it as close to the surface as possible, slowly drop it into the water. Gently push the egg white over the yolk; this may take several passes. Cook for 4 minutes. Remove egg from pan and place into bowl with cold water bath to wash off vinegar and stop the cooking. Remove from cold water with a slotted spoon and trim loose white edges with a knife.**

5. **Arrange waffles on plates. Layer on smoked salmon, then spoon poached egg on top. Garnish with chopped herbs.**

A Garden to Inspire

Truth be told, I found my creativity in the garden. Never really excelling in traditional art classes, I had no idea I had the ability to combine colors and textures to create pleasing color palates. I learned about the importance of depth and variation in height within your composition, which adds visual interest and keeps the eye moving—yes, even in the garden.

It didn't come to me immediately but emerged when I was able to garden in the ground at my first home. I realized I saw plant combinations differently than others—that even if I didn't know the Latin name of a plant {or the common name, for that matter}, I still had a sense of where to place it where it would look great and have a good chance of survival. Every garden is a work in progress, and testing is part of the process, so, yes, I have and still do lose the occasional plant to heat or too much water, but overall my average is pretty good

I could stare at plants for days, inspecting the leaf texture or the shape of the flower. In my garden, I feel personally connected to the plants and responsible for their well-being. When I started to care for others' gardens and study how varieties change through the season, I became more interested in the color variations of each plant and how to mix them within a bed or container.

I believe that we are meant to get our hands dirty every now and then, and although we cannot all have large expansive gardens, we can all have gardens to be proud of: ones that inspire creativity, connect us with nature, and grow our foods when possible. Mother Nature is truly the best artist I have ever encountered; her work is ever-changing and a daily miracle.

Container gardens allow everyone to have a green thumb. Use them at your entranceway to welcome others or to be admired by those passing by. Add plants with various textures, colors, and heights to give the eye many aspects to wander on. Replace annual plants and flowers seasonally to freshen up your entranceway.

Fresh & Simple

The bounty of the summer season at first feels as though it will never arrive, and then, just like that, the tomato bushes are in need of support from falling over due to the weight of their heavy fruit. The basil plants are racing to catch up, and the entire garden is bursting with goodness just waiting to be picked.

This is the time for casual meals eaten outside, culinary creations developed by Mother Nature's schedule, and flavors that tempt you into eating the same dish over and over because you just can't get enough {or you need to eat them before they go to waste}.

Our gardens and roadside markets tempt us to buy ingredients that we have never heard of {but are drawn to just the same} and mounds of berries in cute little blue boxes. Fresh herbs call our names. Dive in. Be curious and daring. You will be glad you did.

On the Menu

Tarragon Herb Butter
Tomato, Goat Cheese, & Chive Tart
Summer Berry Bar
Rosemary Sipper

Tarragon Herb Butter

Occasionally, I have been known to overbuy herbs at the farmers market or overplant the herb containers during the growing season, so during these times I love to make batches of herb butter to use in our meals and also to give as gifts to neighbors or anyone who stops by.

This recipe features tarragon, which I find complements many summer flavors, but you can really use any fresh herbs you have on hand. I find adding a little parsley is a good companion to most herbs.

Ingredients

Makes 1 stick of herb butter

8 tablespoons **unsalted butter, room temperature {1 stick}**
1 teaspoon **kosher sea salt**
1 tablespoon **parsley, minced**
1 tablespoon **tarragon, minced**
Freshly ground black pepper
Salt

Method

1. In a medium bowl, combine room temperature butter, salt, and herbs. Mix until completely blended and creamy.

2. Place soft butter mixture on parchment paper in a line. Roll up mixture into paper to form a tube shape. Chill 30 minutes, then unroll and reroll into a smooth, neat tube. Chill 1 hour minimum or overnight.

Tomato, Goat Cheese, & Chive Tart

Traditionally, a savory tart has a custard-style base, but this version is lighter, super easy, and delivers just as much flavor as its heavier cousin, all while letting the luscious tomato be the star. And one of my favorite things about this tart is it is just as easy to make as it is pretty on the plate! You know I love that!

Ingredients

Serves 6 to 8

1 sheet **puff pastry**
2 tablespoons **olive oil, plus extra**
2 medium **heirloom tomatoes, sliced**
1 small **roll fresh goat cheese**
1 small bunch **chives, chopped**
Freshly ground black pepper
Coarse salt

Method

1. Defrost puff pastry in refrigerator overnight, and roll it out slightly to even and loosen the dough. Slice full sheet into two sections. Brush top lightly with olive oil. Cook puff pastry on a parchment paper–lined baking sheet at 400°F for 15 minutes. Remove pastry from oven.

2. In a small bowl, place sliced tomatoes, olive oil, salt, and pepper, and toss to coat tomatoes. Line tomatoes down the center of pastry and top each slice with 1 teaspoon of goat cheese and pepper. Bake for an additional 10 minutes or until edges of pastry are golden.

3. Top with chopped chives and coarse salt. Slice into sections and serve immediately.

When the summer entertaining season is upon us, it is as if Mother Nature planned it perfectly with the juicy summer berry season. What a fantastic combination! And what better place to combine this match made in heaven than on the cocktail bar.

Strawberries, blackberries, blueberries, and red raspberries placed in small bowls or low dishes provide the perfect colors and flavors to add to a variety of spirits. Your guests' tastes are sure to vary, so be sure to provide two to four spirits including, vodka, rum, bourbon, and gin. Provide a large bowl of ice, a wooden muddler, and plenty of rocks glasses. Arrange a variety of fresh-cut citrus on a cutting board or plate for muddling together.

Create a few small arrangements using clippings from the garden in julep cups to liven up your tray and prepare to greet your warm-weather revelers.

Ingredients

Makes One Cocktail

6 to 10 **rosemary leaves**
4 **fresh raspberries, plus more for garnish**
3/4 ounce **fresh lime juice**
1/2 ounce **simple syrup {see page 107}**
1 1/2 ounces **high-quality gin**
2 ounces **tonic water, add more to taste**
Ice
Rosemary sprig, for garnish
Lime slice, for garnish

Method

1. **In a stainless steel cocktail shaker, muddle finely chopped rosemary leaves, 4 raspberries, and lime juice. Add simple syrup and gin, top with ice, and shake vigorously. Pour into rocks glass over ice and top with tonic water.**

2. **Garnish with rosemary sprig, sliced lime, and raspberries.**

A Birthday Celebration

In my family, your birthday is your day, and I am lucky enough for mine to be during the summer, which always meant sleepovers in the tent in the backyard or up in the attic with every kind of junk food imaginable. I love that my parents always made birthday celebrations so special.

On or about my thirteenth birthday, I was, once again, to host my annual sleepover, but this year's dinner would be different—a special treat usually reserved for the adult parties. The invites went out, and the gorgeous copper and brass pots where polished in anticipation. I was going to have a fondue party! Cheese for the main course and chocolate for dessert—I felt incredibly grown up. Of course it was a huge hit, and all my friends loved it!

It was a special day for me not just because of my birthday and the lovely food but because of the care and presentation that was put into that meal. I now have the smaller of the two fondue pots sitting on my dining room hutch, and I bring it out occasionally for parties and get-togethers, each time taking the same care as my mother took that summer day on the screened-in porch of my childhood home.

Never underestimate the value of the extra time you take to create a pretty table or prepare a wonderful meal; it will be recognized and remembered by your family or guests for years to come. I promise.

On the Menu

Cheese Fondue
Assorted Crudite
Chelada

When I was younger, we lived overseas, traveled extensively, and experienced different cultures and their diverse cuisines. When we returned to the States, my mom would still make a few of the recipes she learned while traveling, and fondue was one of those. Usually prepared for an adult dinner party, we would watch as she prepped all the ingredients and polished the pots until they sparkled.

Ingredients

Serves 6 to 8

1/2 pound **imported Swiss cheese, shredded**
1/2 pound **Gruyere cheese, shredded**
1 tablespoon **cornstarch**
1 clove **garlic, peeled**
1 cup **dry white wine**
1 tablespoon **lemon juice**
2 tablespoons **kirsch {cherry brandy}**
Pinch nutmeg

Assorted Items to Dip:
  * **Cubed bread or crusty rolls**
  * **Cherry tomatoes**
  * **Granny Smith apples**
  * **Lightly boiled new potatoes**
  * **Raw or roasted vegetables, such as fennel, broccoli, cauliflower, zucchini, and asparagus**
  * **Proteins, such as seared cubed beef or chicken**

Method

1. **In a small bowl, coat the cheeses with cornstarch and set aside.**

2. **Rub the inside of the ceramic fondue pot with the garlic clove, then discard.**

3. **Over medium heat, add the wine and lemon juice and bring to a gentle simmer. Gradually stir the cheese into the simmering liquid. Melt the cheese in gradually to encourage a smooth fondue.**

4. **Once smooth, stir in cherry brandy and nutmeg.**

5. **Bring fondue to a simmer and cook, stirring, until thickened, 5 to 8 minutes. Transfer to fondue pot set over a flame. Set the fondue on the table and serve with bread cubes and fondue forks for dipping.**

Chelada

This beer-based cocktail is popular in Mexico, and, in fact, I had my first one many years ago in a small Mexican town on the gulf. I overheard a local order it, and I had to have one. It was cold and refreshing, just what I needed as a break from the heat. If you add anything to this basic Chelada recipe, it becomes a Michelada; additions include assorted sauces, spices, peppers, and tomato juice. I recommend trying this classic recipe first, then add on as you wish.

Ingredients

Makes One Chelada

1/4 cup **ice**
1 cup **fresh lime juice**
12 ounces **Mexican beer**
Lime wedges, for garnish
Coarse salt, optional

Method

1. **Moisten rim of glass with a lime wedge and coat with coarse salt. Add ice, lime juice, and beer.**

2. **Serve with the bottle of remaining beer and additional lime wedges.**

Crab Feast

Crab could easily be my favorite food, but not in crab cakes or from a tin can, only when hand-cracked over newspaper and picked for hours do they hold the same sweet flavor. To me, a crab feast is the epitome of a summer gathering.

You know you will be there for hours, fingers messy with Old Bay, and you don't mind. In fact, you are looking forward to sharing a table, the bushel of crabs, a few craft beers, great stories, and the afternoon with friends.

And then there is the corn. During the summers living in Connecticut, we would frequently host barbeques at our house. I recall my job, as one of the kids, was to husk the corn. I would sit on the stairs with a bushel of corn and a paper grocery bag with the sides folded over to keep it standing open, content for the moment removing the green husk and yellow silk.

A few of the kids resisted and thought of it as a chore, but I relished those moments. Sitting there on the steps of the back porch, welcoming each new guest as they arrived, smelling the freshness of the sweet corn, unwrapping each new ear to see if it would have more white or more yellow kernels, and then, finally, after it had been cooked, tasting those sweet nuggets with butter dripping down my chin. . . . Now that is what summer is all about!

On the Menu

Steamed Blue Crabs, Maryland Style
New Potatoes with Tarragon Herb Butter
Grilled Corn & Summer Coleslaw
Fresh-Picked Summer Berries

Steamed Blue Crabs, Maryland Style

There are thousands of ways to prepare crabs, and I am sure they are all delicious in their own right; however, I believe many of our preferences for flavors, recipes, and techniques are tied to those we experienced growing up. To me, steamed crabs with Old Bay {frequently referred to as Maryland Style} is the essence of every summer growing up and is still my favorite way to prepare them. Frequently, you can ask to have them steamed in this style at the shop where you are ordering them, but if you are lucky enough to have caught them yourself, this recipe is tried and true, and tested over many generations.

Ingredients

Makes 1 Dozen Crabs

1 dozen **live blue crabs**
1/2 cup **Old Bay Seasoning**
White vinegar
Water

Method

1. **In a pot with a raised rack {minimum of 2 inches high}, add equal quantities of water and vinegar to just below level of rack. Bring to a boil.**

2. **Carefully layer crabs on rack and sprinkle each layer with Old Bay. Cover and steam 20 to 30 minutes {depending on size of crabs}, or until crabs turn red.**

3. **Serve immediately!**

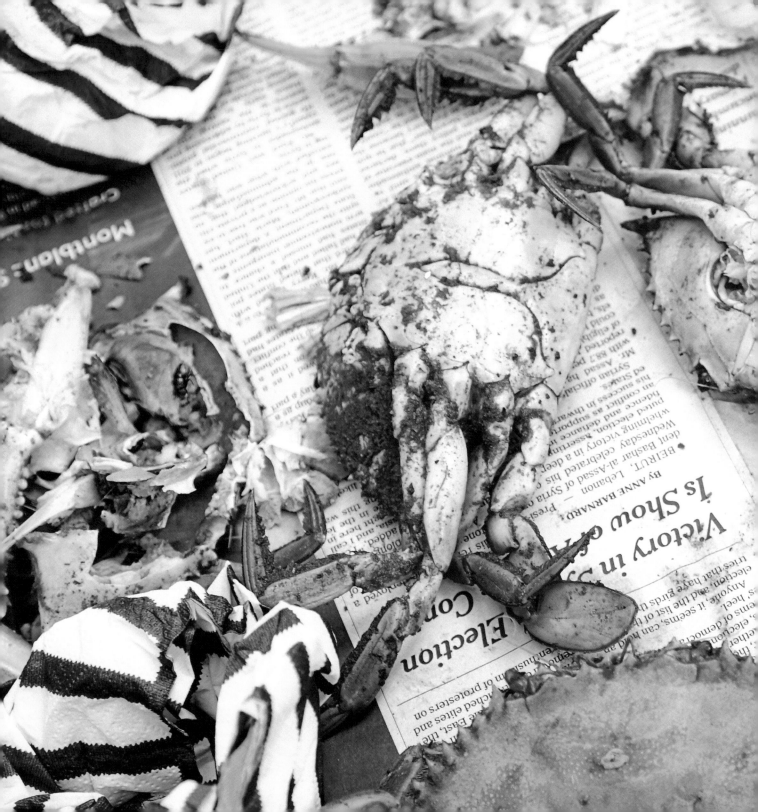

New Potatoes & Grilled Corn with Tarragon Herb Butter

New potatoes are freshly harvested young, or small, potatoes, best in the spring or summer. They have thin skins, and because they are new, they hold lots of moisture inside and also tend to be sweeter than older potatoes. New potatoes are perfect in recipes without a lot of other ingredients, such as potato salad or, my favorite, simply boiled with a bit of herb butter.

Whenever possible, grill your corn as opposed to boiling it. The grilling process brings out a smoky sweetness that makes it well worth the extra effort, and you will not be disappointed. By first soaking the corn with husks on in water, it creates a natural steaming system and also protects the ears from the direct flame.

Ingredients

Serves 6 to 8

1 1/2 pounds **small, white new potatoes**
1 1/2 pounds **small, red new potatoes**
5 to 6 tablespoons **Tarragon Herb Butter**
   {see page 71}
Kosher salt
Freshly ground black pepper

Grilled Corn:
8 ears **corn**
Kosher salt

Method

1. **Rinse any dirt off potatoes and put them into a large pot. Cover with cool water, and generously add salt to water. Cook, gently boiling, until the potatoes are fully tender, 10 to 15 minutes.**

2. **Drain the potatoes into a colander, shaking off as much water as possible. Transfer the potatoes to a serving dish and top with Tarragon Herb Butter. Gently mix to cover all potatoes. Serve warm.**

3. **To prepare the corn, pull the outer husks down the ear to the base and strip away the silk. Fold husks back into place, and place the ears of corn in a large pot of cold water with 1 tablespoon of salt for 15 minutes.**

4. **Remove corn from water and place on a preheated grill. Grill covered for 15 to 20 minutes, turning every 5 minutes or so.**

5. **Remove corn from the heat and peel back to remove the husks. Spread herb butter over the corn while hot.**

Autumn

Step into Fall

Autumn has a special place in my heart when it comes to filling the home and table with elements of the season. Seasonal decorating begins to hit its stride, and Mother Nature's palette evolves into the more mature colors of autumn. Leaf peeping becomes a weekend pastime, and corn fields are mown into mazes, just waiting for a hay wagon full of visitors to conquer its puzzling paths. Even the grocery stores are ready, with displays overflowing with a rainbow of mums, wooden cases full of pumpkins in every shape and size, and the ever-present aroma of cinnamon pinecones that seems to cling to you hours after you walk by them.

Begin showcasing the bounty of the season at your entranceway. Pumpkins, gourds, ornamental cabbage, and Indian corn are in abundance, making them an affordable way to decorate inside and out. Look for heirloom varieties, which seem to last longer than those conventionally produced. They come in such incredible shapes and colors, so don't be afraid to stray from the usual, perfectly round, orange pumpkin. I love combining the less common green varieties with Cinderella and Blue Hubbards at my entranceway for an unexpected display.

As the days begin to shorten, you may need to call on the assistance of lanterns to provide additional lighting at the door or on the table. Warm wood and the golden tones of copper and brass perfectly reflect the flickering light. Consider combining various heights to create an inviting display on a front porch step or repeating the same shape down the center of a table.

As I am not one for placing a standard wreath on the door, I could not resist the inherent beauty of this Black Beard wheat pattern {left} when I saw it on display. Continue the feeling into your living spaces by filling ceramic bowls or glass vases with dried leaves or other elements found on afternoon walks.

Sunday Dinner

After a weekend of running around, it is comforting to be at home and regroup before the workweek begins again. Sunday dinner is a time to reconnect with yourself and family, so keep this time stress-free by setting the table with peaceful colors and serving your favorite recipes with ingredients from a quick trip to the market or items you picked up over your weekend travels.

When it is just the two of us for dinner, we sit in the kitchen, and if we are in a larger group, we like to spread out at the farm table and reflect on events of the past few days, storytelling, laughing, and occasionally embellishing the details of our memories.

Let the season dictate what you serve and how you serve it—light and fresh for spring or aromatic and hearty for autumn. Continue this feel with the table settings and napkins. For the flowers, I love to pick up a fresh bouquet at the Saturday farmers market when I can and let its seasonal colors create the palette for the week's tablescape.

On the Menu

Salmon with Crispy Skin
Green Beans with Almonds & Brown Butter

Salmon with Crispy Skin

Salmon is one of my favorite types of fish, so I am always looking for new tasty ways to prepare it. I discovered the crispy-skin style while I was event planning for a caterer in Bucks County; it was on the menu for a private dinner I was working on, and the chef prepared it perfectly—I was hooked.

The first time I made it at home, my husband acted like I was some sort of kitchen goddess. Needless to say, it is now the most commonly prepared dish in my home.

Ingredients

Serves 6

Avocado Oil
6 {6-ounce} pieces center-cut salmon fillet
with skin, about 1-inch thick
Coarse kosher salt
Freshly ground black pepper
2 tablespoons lemon juice

Method

1. Place oven rack approximately 7 inches from the heat source. Preheat oven on high broil.

2. Sprinkle the salmon, skin-side up, with lemon juice and generous amounts of salt and pepper.

3. On the stovetop, heat an oven-safe pan to medium-high. Add avocado oil to barely coat the bottom.

4. Place the fish in the pan skin-side up and cook on medium-high for 5 to 7 minutes, or until you can see that 1/4 of the thickness is cooked through.

5. Transfer the pan with the salmon, skin-side up, into the oven. Cook until the skin is crispy and the fish is cooked through, 7 to 8 minutes.

{Note: This style is easy and quick but whenever using the broiler, be sure to stay in the kitchen to oversee the cooking.}

Green Beans with Almonds & Brown Butter

It is true that brown butter can make anything taste better, but when it is combined with fresh green beans and toasted almonds, it elevates this classic by adding richness to a basic vegetable. This recipe is really wonderful in autumn when we are looking for foods that add a layer of warmth to the menu without too much additional time in the preparation.

Ingredients

Serves 6

2 pounds **fresh green beans, washed and trimmed**
4 tablespoons **butter**
1 cup **slivered almonds, toasted**
Salt
Freshly ground black pepper
Water

Method

1. **Place a wide-bottomed skillet over medium heat. Add the butter {it will become almost frothy}, and continue to heat while monitoring it. When the melted butter turns golden brown and releases the aroma of toasting nuts, stir in the almonds. This will lower the butter's temperature and stop it from burning.**

2. **Continue cooking, stirring the almonds as they heat through and gently toast, approximately 5 minutes.**

3. **To the same pan, add green beans, salt, pepper, and a splash of water. Toss well to coat the beans with the butter and nuts. Cover the pan with a lid, lower the heat to medium-low, and continue cooking, steaming the beans until they're tender, approximately 7 to 10 minutes.**

Game-Day Grilling

Summer's warm days may have passed, but that doesn't mean the grill needs to be tucked away just yet; in fact, these are the best months to use the grill! Autumn's cooler temperatures are perfect for the heartier flavors we associate with grilling, such as sage, smoke, and mesquite. Dry rubs are amazing on meats and poultry but also add a bold flavor to fish and vegetables.

Game day is the perfect time to use all those big platters and serving pieces you have stashed away. Load them up with skewers of fresh vegetables, toasted rolls from the corner bakery, and toppings galore. Let your guests grab a cold beverage and something off the grill, and create their ideal combination of flavors; it requires less work from you and everyone is free to mingle around the warmth of the fire before heading in to catch the second half.

On the Menu

Grass-Fed Burgers
Elevated Condiment Tray
Arnold Palmer with Fresh Mint

Grass-Fed Burgers & Elevated Condiment Tray

The good old-fashioned American hamburger. Truth be told, having given up red meat many years ago, this isn't a recipe for me—it's for all the carnivores in my life who salivate at the first whiff of grass-fed beef kissed by hardwood charcoal.

As for me, it's all about the condiment tray. Some may think of this as merely a plate of lettuce and tomatoes, but I cannot count the number of times the condiment tray has saved the day. I have {more than once} made entire meals for parties or tailgates from this tray of vegetables, cheeses, and spreads, so don't be afraid to elevate your standard array by offering several cheeses, a variety of heirloom tomatoes, and a selection of mustards. Your vegetarian friends will enjoy it just as much as the burger crowd.

Ingredients

Serves 6 to 8

1 medium *yellow onion, coarsely grated*
2 pounds *grass-fed ground beef*
2 teaspoons *parsley, finely chopped*
1 1/2 teaspoons *salt, plus more*
1/2 teaspoon *freshly ground black pepper, plus more*
12 *pretzel or brioche buns, toasted*

Condiment Tray:
  * *Candied or spicy bacon strips*
  * *Assorted heirloom tomatoes*
  * *Cheese: blue, Swiss, aged cheddar*
  * *Caramelized onions*
  * *Red onion*
  * *Romaine lettuce ribs*
  * *Mayonnaise*
  * *Mustard*
  * *Ketchup*

Method

1. Heat grill to medium-high heat.

2. Using clean hands, in a large bowl combine onion, grass-fed beef, salt, and pepper. Gently shape into six loosely formed 1 1/2-inch-thick round patties. Using your thumb, press a deep thumbprint, nearly halfway through, in the center on the top side of each patty.

3. Season patties with salt and pepper, and place on grill. Cook 4 to 6 minutes per side for medium-rare. Serve on buns with desired toppings.

Arnold Palmer with Fresh Mint

Reportedly invented in the 1960s when golf legend Arnold Palmer ordered this drink at lunch and a woman overheard him ordering it and preceded to order "the Palmer Drink," this refreshing combination of iced tea and lemonade is ideal for beating the heat. This recipe calls for fresh-squeezed lemon juice and simple syrup. How can I get a drink named after me?

Ingredients

Serves 4 to 6

8 **English breakfast tea bags**
8 cups **boiling water**
1 cup **simple syrup {see below}**
1 cup **lemon juice**
1 **lemon, zest**
Ice cubes
4 cups **water**

Simple Syrup:
1 cup **sugar**
1 cup **water**

Method

1. **For the tea:** Tie the tea bags together and attach to the handle of a large heat-proof pitcher. Pour the hot water over the tea bags and into the pitcher. Set aside to steep for 5 minutes. Remove and discard the tea bags and chill tea in the refrigerator until ready to serve.

2. **For the simple syrup:** Add the sugar and water to a medium saucepan. Bring to a boil and allow to simmer until the sugar has dissolved. Remove from the heat and set aside to cool completely.

3. **For the lemonade:** In a blender, add the simple syrup, lemon juice, lemon zest, and ice cubes and pulse to puree. Add water, then place the mixture into a pitcher.

4. **Add ice cubes to a large glass, then fill half with the tea and top with lemonade.**

A Harvest Party

Sometimes there is no better reason to host a party other than simply the desire to bring friends together and share a meal. I am part of a wine club that was created for this exact reason. Each month, we rotate houses, taking turns hosting to share the work of preparing. Lucky for me, I drew an autumn month and was able to set the table in a harvest theme complete with amazing produce from the market and some of my favorite dinnerware.

White Wedgwood china banded in a burnished platinum and topped with a pure-white cotton dinner napkin wrapped in a dried grapevine holder paired perfectly with the natural tones on the wood farm table and elements lining the center.

For the centerpiece, I started with a burlap runner covering the entire length of the ten-foot table, then placed three Napa Valley–inspired lanterns with white candles down the center to create a grounding element. Fading green hydrangeas and maroon mums were gently tucked into groupings of Turks Turban gourds, green-grey artichokes, and purple variegated graffiti eggplants.

On the Table

Natural Elements of the Season
White China & Cotton Napkins
A Variety of Wines for Tasting

A few favorite books act as trivets for a cabbage-leaf-textured covered serving bowl, and silver wine coasters protect the table from red wine rings. The scene is set for a wine tasting, complete with a several-course meal, each prepared by wine club members to be shared with friends.

Thanksgiving

I believe that, generally speaking, people fall into one of two categories when it comes to Thanksgiving Day: either you prefer to be hosted or you prefer to host. I have done both, and, shockingly, I prefer to host, for two simple reasons: setting the table and having leftovers.

It's the Super Bowl of autumn tablescapes! Gourds dream of being in the big show. Plates, stemware, and napkins pray to be pulled off the bench to make an appearance. This is the table you have practiced your entire year for. Do not hold back. Pull out all the stops, but don't make the mistake of overcrowding; be sure you leave enough free space for the turkey and all the trimmings that accompany it.

I prefer to set the table the day before; most advise this to reduce the number of responsibilities you have on Thanksgiving and also to ensure that you have the all proper serveware cleaned and laid out. These are all valid reasons, but, honestly, I set it so I can have longer to admire it. Lets face it—on Thursday, you are either in the kitchen or visiting with guests; there is not much time to marvel at your autumnal masterpiece.

On the Menu

The Perfect Roast Turkey
Winter Squash Soup
Roasted Brussels Sprouts
Rustic Mashed Potatoes
Fall Fig Harvest Cocktail

The Perfect Roast Turkey

Believe it or not, cooking a turkey is actually much easier than most people think. To serve the perfect bird, the work begins when you purchase it. To ensure plenty of leftovers, allow 1 1/2 pounds of turkey per person; the minimum size should be ten pounds. If you think you will need less, consider buying a breast. Thanksgiving is a time for visitors, so consider how many guests you will need to feed in the days after and adjust accordingly.

Ingredients

Serving Size Depends on Turkey Size

1 turkey, **any size {adjust seasoning as needed}**
2 cloves **garlic, peeled**
1 sprig **rosemary, more for garnish**
1 orange, **sliced in half**
5 tablespoons **herb butter {see page 71}**
Freshly ground black pepper
Course kosher salt

Method

1. **About an hour before roasting, take the fresh or completely defrosted turkey out of the fridge. Remove any packaging as well as the bag of giblets {check in the body cavity and in the neck cavity}. Set the turkey breast-side up on the roasting rack, and let it sit for 1 hour to come up to room temperature.**

2. **Preheat the oven to 450°F.**

3. **Inside the cavity of the turkey, place garlic cloves, rosemary sprig, and orange. Under the skin, place herb butter, distributing it evenly side to side. Finally, on the outside skin, season with salt and pepper. Place the turkey in the oven and brown for 10 minutes. Turn down the heat to 350°F.**

4. **Cooking time: The general rule for cooking a turkey is 13 minutes per pound. Start checking the temperature of your turkey halfway through the scheduled cooking time to gauge how fast it is cooking. Every 45 minutes, remove the turkey from the oven and baste the turkey all over.**

5. **Check the temperature of the turkey in three places: the breast, the outer thigh, and the inner thigh. In each spot, the meat should be at least 165°F. If any area is under temperature, cover the breast meat, wings, and legs with foil to keep from overcooking, and put the turkey back in the oven for another 20 minutes.**

6. **When the turkey is up to temperature, remove from oven, transfer to a cutting board, and let rest for 25 to 30 minutes before slicing.**

Winter Squash Soup

As much as I love to use winter squash to decorate a table, I love it even more prepared as an ingredient. The combination of butternut and acorn squash with sage and nutmeg is one of the most comforting combinations I have ever tasted. This soup is gorgeous served as a first course in toasted acorn squash bowls.

Ingredients

Serves 8

3 tablespoons **good-quality olive oil**
3/4 teaspoon **kosher salt**
1/2 teaspoon **freshly ground black pepper**
3 tablespoons **unsalted butter**
1 tablespoon **good-quality olive oil**
2 cups **yellow onion, chopped**
1 1/2 pounds {about 4 cups} **acorn squash, peeled and chopped**
1 1/2 pounds {about 4 cups} **butternut squash, peeled and chopped**
3 {14.5-ounce} packages **low-salt chicken broth**
2 teaspoons **kosher salt**
1/2 teaspoon **freshly ground black pepper**
1 1/4 teaspoons **fresh sage, finely chopped**
1 teaspoon **ground nutmeg**
1/4 cup **whipping cream**
Grated Gruyere cheese

Method

1. Heat the butter and oil in a heavy-bottomed stockpot, then add the onion and cook over medium heat until translucent {about 10 minutes}.

2. Add the acorn squash, butternut squash, chicken stock, salt, and pepper. Cover and simmer over medium heat for about 20 minutes, until the squash is very tender.

3. Transfer to a food processor {or carefully use an immersion blender} and puree until smooth. Return to pot, add the sage, nutmeg, and cream, and heat slowly. Add salt and pepper to taste.

4. Top with grated Gruyere cheese and serve hot with whole sage leaf garnishes, if desired.

Roasted Brussels Sprouts

I have to admit, I didn't like Brussels sprouts growing up. Does anyone? However, I fell in love with them when I saw them growing in the garden. They are cute little cabbages emerging from a hearty stalk into an amazing spiral, truly an inspiring design by Mother Nature. A simple treatment of olive oil, salt, and pepper is all that is needed to bring out their earthy goodness.

Ingredients

Serves 6 to 8

1 1/2 pounds **Brussels sprouts**
3 tablespoons **good-quality olive oil**
3/4 teaspoon **kosher salt**
1/2 teaspoon **freshly ground black pepper**

Method

1. Wash and rinse Brussels sprouts, then cut off the brown ends and pull off any yellow outer leaves.

2. Preheat oven to 350°F.

3. In a large saucepan, blanch the Brussels sprouts in rapidly boiling salted water for 6 to 8 minutes. Remove with slotted spoon and drain completely.

4. Mix Brussels sprouts in a bowl with olive oil, salt, and pepper. Pour into roasting pan and roast for 20 to 25 minutes, until crisp on the outside and tender on the inside. Shake the pan from time to time to brown the sprouts evenly.

5. Sprinkle with more kosher salt and serve immediately.

Rustic Mashed Potatoes

Snowy white potatoes are a tradition in my family. They are rich and creamy, look pretty on the table, and are always a huge hit. But what happens when, as a young girl, you were told by a wise man {or perhaps it was a family friend giving a little girl a hard time} that if you don't eat the potato skins, your hair will turn super curly and frizzy {just like his}? You grow up thinking that eating the skins is a must, or else! So, when it comes to my mashed potatoes, skins are in. This recipe is a more rustic version and promises to give your hair the perfect amount of wave.

Ingredients

Serves 6 to 8

5 pounds **medium russet potatoes, cleaned**
2 cups **half-and-half**
1/2 cup **crème fraîche**
1 tablespoon **salt, plus more for water**
10 tablespoons **unsalted butter, cut into 1/2-inch pieces, room temperature**
Freshly ground black pepper
Fresh parsley, chopped, plus more for topping

Method

1. Slice clean potatoes into quarters and place into a large stock pot, cover with water, add salt, and bring to a boil on high heat. Reduce the heat to medium-low and simmer until the potatoes are tender when pierced with a skewer or toothpick, 20 to 25 minutes.

2. Drain water in a colander and return potatoes to pot. Add the half-and-half, and, using a hand potato masher, mash until smooth with some lumps. Mix in butter. Mash again until combined.

3. Add crème fraîche, parsley, salt, and pepper. Mix with a wooden spoon until smooth. Season to taste with salt and pepper.

Fall Fig Harvest Cocktail

This twist on the champagne cocktail recipe has a touch of warm fig, which adds just the right amount of depth to stand up to the bolder flavors of autumn. Welcoming guests to a Harvest or Thanksgiving dinner with this cocktail will soon to be a seasonal tradition.

Add a splash of bourbon to further warm up the flavor in this cocktail.

Ingredients

Makes One Cocktail

1 to 2 teaspoons **Sweetened Fig Puree** {see below}
Champagne
Splash of bourbon {or to taste}

Sweetened Fig Puree:
1/4 cup **water**
1/2 cup **sugar**
2 whole **fresh figs, quartered**

Method

1. **First, make the Sweetened Fig Puree. In a small pot, combine water and sugar and heat on medium heat until sugar is dissolved. Add figs and reduce heat to low. With an immersion blender, break down figs and blend with sugar and water. Heat for 10 minutes on low. Strain and discard fig solids. Cool puree prior to use in cocktail.**

2. **In a prechilled champagne flute, place up to 2 teaspoons of Sweetened Fig Puree and a splash of bourbon. Slowly add chilled champagne.**

Leftovers

The party is over, but the guests remain, and they are a surprisingly hungry group! Luckily, your fridge is stocked full of leftovers to feed them well. Bobbie Sandwiches—turkey, cranberry relish, stuffing, and mayo served on a hoagie roll—have been a tradition for years; I even crave them during the "off season." But when you are looking to feed a large group something a little different, putting out a bowl of soup and all the fixings is the way to go.

Most likely, your table will already be filled with stacked, cleaned dishes, serving trays, and glassware from the day before, so set out the buffet on a kitchen counter or sideboard for the gang to help themselves. Wooden bowls and natural colors will keep the feel rustic and mood relaxed, which is perfect for chilling out on the couch until everyone is ready for a second helping.

On the Menu

Turkey Tortilla Soup
Variety of Garnishes

Turkey Tortilla Soup

For several years, I commuted to work in New York, and the team in the showroom would always make it a point to keep our lunch schedules open on Tuesdays. Tuesday was the only day Houston's served their Chicken Tortilla Soup, and, believe me, you did not want to miss it! This is my take on their recipe. The masa flour adds depth of flavor to the soup base, but if you have trouble finding it, use additional ground tortillas.

Ingredients

Serves 10

1/4 cup **masa flour**
6 ounces **corn tortilla chips, crushed**
1 1/2 tablespoons **ground cumin**
1 1/2 tablespoons **ground chili powder**
1/2 tablespoon **freshly ground black pepper**
1/4 cup **butter**
1/4 cup **olive oil**
1 large **onion**
1/4 cup **garlic, minced**
4 quarts **chicken stock**
1/4 cup **chicken base**
4 cups **turkey, shredded**
1/4 cups **fresh cilantro, chopped**
Salt and freshly ground black pepper

Garnishes:
  * *Sliced avocado*
  * *Sliced limes*
  * *Monterey Jack cheese, shredded*
  * *Fresh cilantro*
  * *Tortilla strips*

Method

1. In medium bowl, mix masa flour, ground tortilla chips, cumin, chili powder, and pepper together.

2. Melt butter in a larger soup pot. Add olive oil, diced onion, and garlic. Sauté on medium only until onions are softened and clarified. Salt lightly.

3. Add the dry mix to the onions. Cook for 10 to 12 minutes, until the raw flavor of the flour is cooked out. Salt lightly. Slowly add the chicken stock and chicken base. Remove from heat.

4. In the pot, blend the mixture with a hand immersion blender or pour into a countertop blender and blend until all of the flour pieces have blended in and the soup is completely smooth.

5. Return the soup pot to the heat. Bring the soup to a boil, and allow to cook/boil/reduce until the soup has thickened slightly and coats the spoon, about 15 to 30 minutes. Salt and pepper to taste.

6. Ladle soup into bowl and top with turkey, juice of lime wedge, and cilantro. Allow guests to garnish as they desire.

Winter

'Tis the Season

Early in December, I put on my Santa's Helper hat and split time between the north and the south, decorating and making sure everyone's homes are perfectly festive and ready for a month of merrymaking. Some will decorate to host a party, and others do it simply for their families. I love every minute of it, sap-stained hands and all.

A few years ago, when I was driving from one client's home to the next, I stumbled upon what seemed to be a Christmas mirage off the side of the road, down a snowy driveway. It was a wooden farm wagon topped with every type of green you could wish for in labeled buckets or cut and stacked on the burlap-covered bed. And the best part? A coffee can marked "pay here" with a plastic lid for an honor system payment. Not only do I love having such an amazing resource for my seasonal decorating, but I love the possibilities that the magic of the holiday season brings.

At your home, fill now-empty garden containers with greens to welcome guests at the door. If you have access to your own greens, use this as a time to prune and shape your evergreens. Mix and match colors and textures, such as blue spruce with white pine, and add an accent of chartreuse variegated arborvitae.

Rosemary trees are quite common this time of year and add a fantastic aroma to a space while also providing fresh herbs during a season when you may not be able to grow them outside. Use these small trees outside under cover or inside in your kitchen accented with a ribbon.

For a natural feel, fill handmade baskets with pinecones and set them alongside the fireplace. For something a little more flashy, combine bright red with metallics. It is okay to mix and match items that at first you might not expect to be placed together; they work perfectly this time of year.

Tree-Trimming Party

Want to know one of my best-kept secrets for getting the house decorated and ready for the holidays? Schedule a party during the first or second week of December! You will be forced to get the decorations out and at least partially set up. Provide tasty snacks and cocktails, and I promise you will have more than enough elves arrive at your door ready to help you finish your decorating.

Keep the menu light and easy to pick at. A charcuterie and cheese plate is a must-have. Serving bite-sized foods that guests can enjoy in between conversations and placing an ornament on the tree is ideal. Set everything out with small plates, extra napkins, and glasses 30 minutes prior to your first guest's arrival, and take that extra time to finish getting ready.

If you can't get the entire house decorated in time, focus on key design elements like a mantel or staircase. Start with a focal point or heirloom, then add green roping accented with pinecones and fresh-cut magnolia or holly leaves tucked in. Don't forget to light the candles and dim the lights right before the first guest rings the bell.

On the Menu

Charcuterie & Cheese Platter
Citrus-Marinated Olives
Chilled Champagne

Charcuterie & Cheese Platter

I would love to say that I follow a true formula when creating a charcuterie tray or a cheese board, but the reality is that we always have a variety of cheeses, olives, and almonds somewhere in the house that can be brought out at any time; in fact, it is a regular occurrence on Sundays during movie time to bring out the platter and munch away until there are only crumbs left. But when company is coming, I do rely on the traditional formula for selecting cheeses and meats. Include a combination of cheeses from each of the main types: cow, goat, sheep, hard, soft, veined, and include meats in an array of cooked, cured, and aged, mixing textures and colors.

Serve with breads, crackers, olives, nuts, and fresh and dried fruits as well as several lovely spreads. The overall look should be bountiful, like a work of art {but not perfectly formed}, when finally assembled. Prepare the platter 30 minutes or so before the first guest's arrival to allow it to come up to room temperature.

Suggestions

Cheeses: **Triple or Double Crème Brie, Aged Cheddar, Aged Gouda, Humboldt Fog, Manchego, Point Reyes Blue, Taleggio**

Charcuterie: **Artisan Salami, Bresaola, Prosciutto di Parma, Soppressata**

Fruits: **Champagne Grapes, Blackberries, Dried Apricots, Figs, Melon, Pears**

Other Favorites: **Fig Jam, Honeycomb, Quince Paste, Marcona Almonds, Olives**

Crackers: **Water Crackers, Crusty Baguette {sliced}**

Amaryllis blooms are the perfect decoration to have on the entranceway table to greet guests. Start your bulbs growing in a staggered series, so you will have a parade of festive blooms all month long. Keepsake ornaments add a personal touch to your tree. I love to recall where each one came from year after year, keeping the memories alive. This night is about great friends and ringing in a joyous season together. Keep it simple and low stress.

Citrus-Marinated Olives

As a small girl, I loved the look of olives: shiny, smooth, and surely dripping with some tasty liquid. They were in the fancy drinks that glamorous women and secretive men drank, so they had to be fantastic, right?

Problem was, I couldn't stand the taste. Frequently, my best friend would eat them as a snack after school, and I would always give one a try, hoping that I suddenly loved their flavor, but no such luck for many, many years. And then one day it happened; the switch was flipped {as I always knew it would} and my olive addiction began.

Ingredients

Makes 4 Cups

4 cups **mixed variety of unpitted olives,
   select an assortment of colors and sizes**
1 cup **light olive oil**
4 large **garlic cloves, thinly sliced**
2 tablespoons **fresh thyme, finely chopped**
2 whole **bay leaves**
1 lemon, zest and juice
1/4 cup **orange juice**
2 slices **of orange peel, approx. 3 inches long,
   using a potato peeler**
1 sprig **rosemary**

Method

1. Drain olives of any brine and rinse.

2. In a small saucepan over low heat, combine oil, garlic, thyme, and bay leaves, and warm to combine flavors until garlic just begins to brown. Remove from heat and add the remaining ingredients. Mix well.

3. In a glass or ceramic bowl, combine the olives and mixture, and stir well to coat. Cover the bowl and marinate the olives for 2 hours at room temperature. Store the olives and mixture in an airtight container in the refrigerator for up to 2 weeks. Bring to room temperature before serving.

Christmas Eve

The most anticipated night of the entire year. Whether you are seven or seventy, on Christmas Eve you can still feel the magic in the air. The weather is crisp and cool outside, but the heat from the fire and the buzz of excitement warms the entire house.

Traditionally, for me, Christmas Eve dinner was a special meal served at a formally set table where guests dress in their holiday best. I have continued this tradition in my home and love to invite enough guests to fill the table and bring out the china and crystal. Remember, elegantly decorating your table to signify this special evening does not have to mean that the evening will have a stuffy feeling.

Christmas crackers are a European tradition and a fun way to decorate the table. Each guest gets one at their place setting, and sometime during dinner each guest holds an end of their neighbor's cracker and pulls until it snaps open and the contents are revealed. Inside are small games or puzzles and, best of all, colorful paper crowns. Of course, everyone is required to wear theirs for the remainder of the evening.

On the Menu

Seared Scallops with Sage Brown Butter
Butternut Squash Risotto
Wine-Poached Pears
Champagne

For a holiday table, combine rich colors of red roses and cranberries with the rough textures of pinecones into one arrangement. This adds a luxurious visual to the table beyond what a standard bouquet can achieve.

An antiqued mirror glass footed bowl filled with cranberries reflects the candlelight and still allows a touch of red to peek through its base. Consider what stage your flowers are in: if they are newly cut and tight, give them warm water to open up a bit before placing on the table.

Create a mini bouquet in the center and then begin to add pinecones around the edge as the final textural element. Lift the rose bouquet up just a bit so they rest on top. Freshly cut magnolia branches tuck nicely between the arrangements and complete the look on the table.

Seared Scallops with Sage Brown Butter

Known as beurre noisette {burr-nwah-ZET} in France, brown butter, or, literally, "hazelnut butter," is butter that is cooked in a pan until it turns a golden-brown color, resulting in a butter with a nutty flavor and coloring of a hazelnut. Truly heaven in a sauté pan, you can drizzle this freely over anything—scallops, filet, butternut squash, even ice cream—and it will elevate any dish.

Ingredients

Serves 6

1 1/2 to 2 pounds **dry sea scallops**
3 teaspoons **unsalted butter**
3 teaspoons **olive oil**
Kosher salt
Freshly ground black pepper

Sage Brown Butter:
6 tablespoons **butter**
1 tablespoon **fresh sage leaves, finely chopped**

Method

1. **First, prepare the scallops. Carefully remove the small side muscle from the scallops with a knife, rinse with cold water, and pat dry. Salt and pepper both sides of the scallops.**

2. **In a large sauté pan, add the butter and oil, and heat on high. When the butter begins to smoke, place the scallops in the pan. Do not allow them to touch. Sear the scallops for 1 1/2 minutes on each side. The scallops will develop a golden crust on each side, but the center should remain translucent when cut.**

3. **For the Sage Brown Butter: In a saucepan over medium heat, cook the butter until it begins to turn brown {butter will foam first to release water, then brown}. Stir in sage and cook, while continuing to stir, until sage is crisp and butter is golden brown.**

4. **To plate, serve the scallops over Butternut Squash Risotto {page 151}, drizzle with Sage Brown Butter, and serve immediately.**

148

Butternut Squash Risotto

For me, butternut squash and the cold weather months go together like cheese and crackers or salt and pepper; they are a natural combination, soul mates. And the warm seasonings and herbs that pair so well with it, like nutmeg and sage, only add to the comforting aromas and textures coming from the kitchen during this festive time of year.

Ingredients

Serves 6

2 cups **butternut squash, unseasoned, cooked {can be frozen and thawed or fresh}**
1 cup **warm water**
1 teaspoon **nutmeg, to taste**
1 quart **low-sodium stock, chicken or vegetable**
2 tablespoons **butter**
2 tablespoons **extra-virgin olive oil**
1/2 cup **shallots, chopped, about 2 large**
2 cups **arborio rice**
1 cup **dry white wine**
1 teaspoon **salt, plus more to taste**
1/2 teaspoon **freshly ground black pepper, plus more to taste**
1 cup **Parmigiano-Reggiano, grated**

Method

1. In a food processor or blender, combine the butternut squash, water, and nutmeg. Blend until smooth. Set aside.

2. Heat the stock in a small, covered saucepan to a simmer, then leave it on low heat.

3. In a heavy-bottomed pot, melt the butter and olive oil, and sauté the shallots on medium-low heat for 10 minutes, until the shallots are translucent but not browned. Add the rice, and stir well. Then, add the white wine and cook for 2 minutes on medium-low heat.

4. To the rice, add 2 full ladles of hot stock, salt, and pepper. Stir and simmer until the stock is absorbed, about 5 to 10 minutes. Continue to add the stock, 1 to 2 ladles at a time, stirring every few minutes. Each time, cook until the rice mixture absorbs the liquid, then add more stock. Continue until the rice is cooked through but al dente, about 30 minutes total from when rice is first added.

5. Add the roasted squash puree and cheese, and mix well. Remove from heat. Season to taste.

6. Just prior to serving, sprinkle with cheese.

Wine-Poached Pears

During my mom's famous dinner parties, you could always count on a fantastic dessert {my sister apparently got the baking gene} to complete the meal. When I asked about her poached pear recipe, she told me that it came from Amy Vanderbilt's Complete Cookbook, first published in 1961. She still has the book, but "it is taped together and must be handled with care."

Turns out, it was the first cookbook my mother ever owned, and it was given to her by my grandmother. But wait, there's more {as if all of those details aren't enough}: the illustrator for the book was a young Andy Warhol. Food, art, and life—such small, wonderful worlds.

Ingredients

Serves 6

3 winter **pears**
2 cups **red wine**
2 cups **water**
1 cup **sugar**
1 **clove**
1-inch piece **cinnamon stick**
2 **star anises**, more for garnish
1 **orange**, sliced

Method

1. **Wash pears. Pare and slice but leave stems intact.**

2. **Combine wine, water, sugar, clove, cinnamon, star anise, and orange in a large glass or enamel saucepan. Place pears in mixture, ensuring they are completely covered with the liquid. Cover and cook over low heat for 30 minutes, or until pears are tender. Move pears to individual dishes.**

3. **Heat liquid mixture on high to reduce and thicken. Drizzle on plate, placing pear on top. Garnish with star anise or oranges.**

{NOTE: I have slightly adapted this recipe: halved pairs versus whole, the addition of star anise, and I replaced lemon with orange, but the essence of the lovely original remains.}

New Year's Open House

You made it! The holiday season officially ends with New Year's Day, and after the last few months of rushing around, shopping, and hosting, you deserve to sit back and relax. But if you are like me, you don't actually want this festive season to be over quite yet—can't we squeeze in just one more reason to get together?

New Year's Day is the ideal day to host an open house. Everyone is moving a little slower, so a flexible arrival time works best, and although your guests may be ready to eat and drink, the rich foods and robust wines of the last few nights are still weighing on most of them. Keeping the menu simple and easy will require less time in the kitchen and lends itself to the free-flowing nature of an open house. Select foods that keep well at room temperature, and set up a self-serve format for both the food and beverages.

On the Menu

The Bloody Mary Bar
Anchovy & Caramelized-Shallot Tart
Homestyle Frittata
Black-Eyed Pea & Kale Salad

The Bloody Mary Bar

Bloody Marys are a tradition in my family and a staple at all our get-togethers. I recall Sunday brunch at my grandparents' home with various pitchers of fresh, homemade mix on the kitchen counter. Aunts and uncles poured tall glasses of zesty tomato juice, adding dashes of this, splashes of that, and a few of these, then stirred it all together with a tall stick of celery.

When I was finally able to move from the virgin version to an adult blend, I began to learn that Bloodies vary not only by family but geographically as well, with each person in need of a different sauce, powder, or vegetable to complete it. And so, we see the beauty of the Bloody Mary Bar, where each guest has the opportunity to select what they like, leave out what they don't, and perhaps try something new.

Setting up the perfect display takes a little planning and preparation, but once it is done, your work is finished. For home entertaining, I recommend placing juice, vodka, and condiments on a counter or table that allows enough space to keep everything together while also allowing room to mix drinks.

Here are my favorite items to set up, but feel free to add according to you and your guests' preferences. Also be sure to provide additional clean ice, glasses, straws, small wooden stirring spoons, and cocktail napkins.

The Must-Haves
V8 Juice {it's a standard and still delicious}
Bloody Mary Mix {premade or homemade}
Vodka {offer two varieties}

The Add-Ons
Sauces: Worcestershire Sauce, Hot Sauce
Condiments & Spices: Horseradish, Celery Seed, Old Bay Seasoning, Fresh-Cracked Pepper
Produce: Cleaned, Halved Celery Stalks; Green Onions {root ends removed}; Hearts of Palm; Cornichons/Gherkins; Pitted Spanish Olives; Lemons Wedges, Lime Wedges

Anchovy & Caramelized-Shallot Tart

I served this once for a brunch, and a good friend, who is very well traveled, told me that it was a "bold move" to serve anchovies to a group. At first, I wasn't sure how to take it, but then I decided that it was a true compliment, especially when I saw him go back for seconds. Believe me, your guests will not be able to resist this salty-sweet combination.

Ingredients

Serves 6 to 8

1 sheet **puff pastry**
8 tablespoons **butter**
1 shallot, **thinly sliced, rings intact**
1 small **yellow onion, thinly sliced, rings intact**
2 tablespoons **light brown sugar**
1 can **anchovies, in olive oil**
1 teaspoon **thyme, finely chopped**

Method

1. **Defrost puff pastry in refrigerator overnight, and roll it out slightly to even and loosen the dough. Slice full sheet into two sections.**

2. **Melt butter in a small saucepan on medium heat. Brush top of the puff pastry lightly with melted butter.**

3. **Cook puff pastry on parchment paper–lined baking sheet at 400°F for 15 minutes. Remove pastry from oven.**

4. **While pastry is cooking, add shallot and onion to melted butter on medium-high heat, and heat until they soften and become translucent, stirring often to ensure even cooking. When shallots begin to become translucent and soft, add brown sugar to pan. Stir until the sugar is fully dissolved and the liquid begins to thicken. Turn heat to low, and monitor to prevent burning.**

5. **Split ingredients between the two pastries and spread onion mixture in the middle of the pastry, leaving approximately 1 inch on all sides. Place anchovies diagonally on top of onion mixture on the pastry. Sprinkle thyme on top.**

6. **Return to oven and bake for an additional 10 minutes or until edges of pastry are golden.**

7. **Slice into sections and serve immediately.**

Homestyle Frittata

A frittata is the ideal recipe to serve for breakfast the morning after a party. The fridge is filled with delicious odds and ends that you may or may not be able to fit into another recipe this week, so chop it all up, mix it with eggs, and almost inevitably you will end up with an incredibly satisfying dish. This lovely version has a fantastic post-party-friendly cheat: potato chips!

Ingredients

Serves 8

4 ounces {about 2 1/4 cups} crushed thick-cut potato chips, like Cape Cod brand
2 ounces thinly sliced prosciutto or bacon, diced
1/3 cup red peppers or chilies, diced
1/3 cup yellow onions, diced
1 tablespoon thyme leaves
8 eggs, lightly beaten
Salt and freshly ground black pepper, to taste
2 tablespoons olive oil

Method

1. In a sauté pan over medium high heat, render the bacon. Once it has released about 2 teaspoons of bacon fat, add the red peppers and onions and sauté until caramelized. Remove from heat and let cool.

2. Heat broiler to high.

3. Combine potato chips, bacon, peppers, onions, thyme, eggs, and salt and black pepper in a bowl, and let sit to allow chips to soften in eggs, about 5 minutes.

4. Heat oil in a 10-inch, nonstick skillet over medium-high heat. Add egg mixture and cook, without stirring, until bottom begins to brown, about 3 minutes. Transfer to broiler and broil until set and golden on top, about 3 minutes. Cut into wedges to serve.

Black-Eyed Pea & Kale Salad

I am, admittedly, a sucker for a good tradition, especially if it is based in prosperity and good energy. So when I heard about the Southern tradition of eating black-eyed peas on New Year's Day, I was determined to find a way to make those little legumes have as much flavor as possible.

The practice of eating black-eyed peas for luck is generally believed to date back to the Civil War and, according to Southern folklore, is the first food to be eaten on New Year's Day for luck and prosperity throughout the year ahead.

Ingredients

Serves 6 to 8

1 cup **black-eyed peas**
2 cups **kale, deribbed and chopped**
1/4 cup **dried apples**
1/4 cup **dried cranberries**
1/4 cup **red onion, finely sliced**

Dressing:
1 tablespoon **fresh lemon juice**
1 teaspoon **sherry vinegar**
2 teaspoons **Dijon mustard**
1 clove **garlic, minced**
2 tablespoons **olive oil**
1 tablespoon **chives, chopped**
Salt and freshly ground black pepper

Method

1. **Whisk dressing ingredients together. Taste, adjust seasonings, and set aside.**

2. **Place chopped kale leaves in a large bowl, and drizzle with a tiny bit of olive oil and a few pinches of salt. Using your hands, rub the leaves together, massaging the kale until it becomes soft and darker in color.**

3. **Combine kale, dried apples, dried cranberries, and red onions in a bowl. Toss with 3/4 of the dressing and let rest for 30 minutes.**

4. **Add the black-eyed peas and toss with the remaining dressing. Taste, adjust seasonings, and serve.**

{NOTE: This is another easy, kitchen-sink kind of salad. Have leftover sweet potatoes or butternut squash? Don't have sherry vinegar? Apple cider or balsamic vinegar are good substitutes.}

Love Potion

When my husband and I were dating, we drank a simple combination of champagne and cranberry juice on the weekends when we where able to spend time together. The story goes that he tricked me into falling in love with him by using the magical powers of this "Love Potion." We aren't sure if this is true or not, but we continue to drink it today so the spell does not wear off.

We are happy to share our Love Potion with you, and we wish you all the love and happiness we have. Pair it with a sweet, bite-sized treat, and serve it to your loved one on a sturdy tray while they are still resting in bed on a Saturday morning.

Spending time with loved ones is one of life's most precious gifts that we frequently take for granted and so often do not do enough. Life passes us by in a second, so be sure to make space in your day to connect with those who mean the most to you, because in the end, love is what this crazy world is all about.

On the Menu

Blinis with Chocolate Hazelnut Spread
Fresh Strawberries
Love Potion Cocktail

Blinis with Chocolate Hazelnut Spread & Fresh Strawberries

Blinis are a traditional Russian pancake made with buckwheat flour and can be used as a base for savory flavors, such as smoked salmon or caviar topped with sour cream, or sweet flavors, like chocolate and strawberries, as in this recipe. Make a few batches ahead of time and then top them right before serving for either a sweet or savory mouthful.

Ingredients

Makes 18 Blinis

1/3 cup **buckwheat flour**
2/3 cup **all-purpose flour**
1/2 teaspoon **baking powder**
3/4 teaspoon **kosher salt**
3/4 cup **milk plus** 2 tablespoons
1 large **egg**
8 tablespoons **unsalted butter, melted**
Chocolate hazelnut spread
Strawberries, finely chopped
Mint, chiffonade cut

Method

1. In a small bowl, combine flours, baking powder, and salt, and whisk together.

2. In a separate medium bowl, whisk milk, egg, and 1 tablespoon of the butter. Add dry flour mixture to milk mixture and whisk to combine. Let batter rest for 5 to 10 minutes.

3. Heat a large nonstick pan or flat griddle over medium heat. Lightly grease pan with butter. Working in batches, drop batter by tablespoonfuls onto pan. Cook until small bubbles appear and pop on top of the batter, about 2 minutes. Flip and cook until browned on both sides, about 1 minute. Repeat the steps using the remaining batter. Freeze unused wrapped blinis in an airtight container.

4. Using a frosting knife, cover the top of each blini with chocolate hazelnut spread and top with strawberry and mint.

The Basics

There are a few items I feel every hostess should have in preparation for a life of celebrations. These are the basics, and I encourage you to start here and build on them. When you see a set of plates or that perfect wine glass in your travels, snatch it up; like designing your home, items on your table should carry memories of different people and places.

12 each of the following:

White China Dinner Plates: Bone china is incredibly strong, resists chipping, and is the perfect white to present your recipe creations on.

Salad or Accent Plates: Have fun with colors and shapes. Mix and match, and use for appetizer, salad, or dessert courses.

Clear Glass Wine Glasses: Uncut red wine glasses are the perfect shape to be used for any style wine or as a water glass to compliment various styles of dinnerware.

Flatware: Silver, gold, or stainless, but be sure you have the full five-piece setting.

Cloth Napkins: White cotton or linen is the easiest to wash and keep clean. Replace if serious stain does occur.

1 or 2 each of the following:

Oversized Platters: Large platters in various shapes make an enormous impact when you are serving guests. Collect them in white, wood, or silver.

Large Serving Bowls: For salads and side dishes. Pick them up in various sizes and depths.

Cake Stand: Not just for desserts; a footed stand elevates cheeses or even a flower arrangement.

Three Tier Server: Perfect for desserts but also for serving on a small table for more intimate gatherings. It takes up less space and is visually appealing.

Vases: Anything that holds water can double as a vase, but having a few in various heights and sizes will encourage you to always have flowers on the table.

Trays: Great for carrying items from the kitchen and creating a focused display. Add a small bud vase or low arrangement for more impact.

For more information regarding entertaining basics, visit www.AnAppealingPlan.com. I have added a section for the basics that will go into further detail.

Acknowledgments

Thank you to all my dear friends and family who patiently listened to my stories and supported me over the year of developing this book. I would like to express my immense gratitude to Heather Stalker, my partner on this roller coaster of a journey—it would not have been possible to create this book without you. We did it!

Special thanks are due to the following companies for providing me with many of the props used in the photographs: Waterford Wedgwood, Fresh Market, and Home Goods.

Thank you to every single person who pledged, told a friend, or shared my Kickstarter project to support the publishing of this book. Due the number of supporters, I have listed their names on the website; however, special love goes to Kickstarter supporters who went above and beyond in their support: Susan Eichert, and Karen Mertes.

Hugs and kitchen love go to my testing team for ensuring my recipes will taste just as good in your kitchen as they do in mine: Angela Bryant, Kristina Campbell, Tami Cunningham, Karen Foy, Tamsen Horton, Cindy Kerschner, Leigh Olson, Debi Price, Dale Rogerson, Amber-Rose Thomas, and Christy Waterhouse.

Gratitude to Lisa Dugger and Shannon Darling for a lifetime of love.

Thank you to Suzanne Perry for saving Christmas in July, and to Dae Sheridan, Scott Sheridan, Liane Caruso, Catherine Pylant, Jaime Kulaga, and James Simmons for showing up and being fabulous.

An honorable mention goes to two absolute gentlemen who not only inspired me with their passion but taught me the importance of artistry and craftsmanship in our lives—Lord Piers Wedgwood and Mr. Jim O'Leary.

And finally, thank you to my clients, who constantly inspire and encourage me to dream in full color. This is for you.

RESOURCES

Balthazar
balthazarny.com

Bobo NYC
bobonyc.com

Carousel Lavender Farm
carouselfarmlavender.com

Cheese Please Tampa
cheesepleasetampa.com

Houston's Restaurants
hillstone.com

Waterford Wedgwood
wwrd.com

BOOKS

Mastering the Art of French Cooking
by Julia Child, Louisette Bertholle, and Simone Beck
Alfred A. Knopf, Random House, Inc., New York, 1961

Amy Vanderbilt's Complete Cookbook
by Amy Vanderbilt
Double Day & Company, New York 1961

PHOTOGRAPHY CREDITS

All photography by Heather Stalker except:
Krayl Funch: pages 13, 42–46, 66, 74, 93–95, 117, 131–133
Brandi Morris: pages 20–23, 65

COPYEDITING

Nicole Wayland of Ford Editing. Thank you for your time and attention to detail.

Index

CPSIA information can be obtained at www.ICGtesting.com
Printed in the USA
BVIW12n0016230217
476896BV00006B/14